COMMODORE
OLIVER HAZARD PERRY

BY

ARTHUR RAYMOND BAUMAN

Library of Congress Catalog Number 96-71264

ISBN Number 1-57087-293-7

Professional Press
Chapel Hill, NC 27515-4371

Manufactured in the United States of America
00 99 98 97 96   10 9 8 7 6 5 4 3 2 1

TABLE OF CONTENTS

INTRODUCTION

In American history, there have been a few moments of historical value that took place, from which mankind received great benefits. In the 20th century, some things that took place seem to have been placed on the back burner, and we show no great interest. But for some of us, we have great enthusiasm to find out what really took place.

My point is about the War of 1812 in the United States of America. There's a place for it in the annals of history, but it lacks the impact of other wars. Most individuals who participate in historical events are considered to be the main actors, but were they merely predestined to be there? I do not know. I feel that some things were meant to happen, to shape our present society and be absorbed into our make-up. Why, during the War of 1812, did some actors become greater than others? I feel that it was the personality involved. Look at Andrew Jackson, who slowly traveled down the Mississippi River on his way to New Orleans, Louisiana. The War of 1812 was over by the time

Andrew Jackson arrived in New Orleans. The British had surrendered, but the information had not reached Jackson, who launched the Battle of New Orleans. Despite this error, Andrew Jackson is still a famous name throughout America for his feats during the War of 1812. But there were other battles that took place with other actors who fulfilled their mission, but never achieved fame as Andrew Jackson. Andrew Jackson went on to become a president of the United States.

I have other interests in the Northern Battles of the War of 1812, in particular the Battle of Lake Erie, starring Commodore Oliver Hazard Perry. I have asked a few people here, and in several places in Ohio, who Commodore Perry was. They replied, "Commodore Who?" I wish, as I sit here in Falls Church, Virginia, that I could have a psychic, metaphysical spiritualist sitting here to conjure up the ghost of Oliver Hazard Perry. I took a lot of valuable time investigating his life at the Library of Congress here in Washington, D.C. I wish that he could sit here on my left side, watching me write about him. Would he smile, thinking of me as somebody looking for an obscure individual who was almost forgotten? Several times I have visited the middle Bass Island, around the Sandusky Bay on the western shore of Lake Erie. There stands a monument in the memory of the Battle of Lake

Erie, along with the names of the men killed in action.

I like the past, and studying the actions of the few actors known for their tenacity and life without fear. My idea of a good soldier is a unique individual—a self-starter who can look up to death as a second friend.

Psychologically, anyone can be trained to do anything, especially at a young age. The formative years are the fortune tellers of what we are going to be. Religion teaches us of predestination, where things were meant to be, good and bad. I am also convinced that some people have good karma, and some have bad karma though most people have mixed karma, because of their choices. I always believe in choice. I chose this life-style, but I do not know what is going to happen next.

I believe that a few people are chosen to become leaders of men. Their place in life was cut out for them, their formative years have events that challenge and stimulate them. Their surroundings seemed to guide them to their goal. Unlike our present society, Oliver Perry lived in a time where communications were poor, where the media didn't provide access to what leaders' actions were really like. Therefore, they got away with things, even embarrassing things just a few people ever saw, but would never harm them in the public eye. But then, most famous people always were good-looking, had normal character personalities, and anything written about them was always good. Nothing was ever written about most people with schizophrenic bouts of insanity. There were a few, but they were the exception. The man that I am writing about always showed a calmness, readiness, and the great tenacity to be a hero. He was a gentleman, an educated New Englander from Rhode Island, who had his career cut out for him, to bring him to fame. But then his life ended in tragedy, with sudden death at a relatively young age. A few weeks ago, when I visited the Library of Congress in Washington, D.C., I painstakingly researched the identity of Commodore Oliver Hazard Perry. There were several manuscripts written about him, but I narrowed my search down to a few distinct historical items in the life and times of Perry.

Some people were meant to do what they did, they were predestined to greatness at an early age. They were attractive, looked at with envy. There was a fascination to the final moments, of everything they said, they wrote, and what they physically did during those special few moments that will change their consciousness, and personality forevermore. That's what I like about life. There's always that magical moment of perfection that takes place, where it was either rehearsed before they lived, or they created the scene as the director of the play. I wish I could be there in those glorious moments where history took place, where it changed the destiny of man.

I also want to mention that during those glorious moments, there is often something negative that surrounds the main actors. There is always that character defect every man has. Or there's someone in the background who has hidden motives—people that dislike themselves, because they have no imagination, or are consumed by jealousy. They always dreamed, and schemed of doing great things, but didn't know how to go about it, nor were they in the right position at the right time, or shall I say, "a matter of coincidence." There are most people that follow like sheep into the slaughter, because of undue respect, because they do not quite understand what to do, they don't know what to think, because they do not know how. King Solomon described mankind very well, 3500 years ago in the books of Ecclesiastics, and Proverbs. What man was like then holds true today in the 20th century. Nothing under the sun has ever changed. But there always are that few people that have the gift to make things happen.

No matter how positive people were, and are today, there also was that hidden enemy that could destroy the destiny of mankind, no matter how great and small. That was and is bacteria. During the early years of the 19th century, life was meager, rough, harsh, and crude. Life was not clean, the constitution of the human body had to be strong to survive severe weather changes in the northern climates, which in turn brought on epidemics, of small pox, influenza, tuberculosis, malaria, dysentery, and pneumonia These were fatal. Here in the 20th century, we tend to romanticize that glorious era of the War of 1812, with clean-cut officers, well dressed in their uniforms, and we tend to ignore the suffering and the mental anguish those people felt. Life was actually a struggle. The War of 1812 was really in its height and glory in Europe, when Napoleon Bonaparte was conquering Central Europe by storming into other territories with his soldiers. Napoleon Bonaparte was a tyrant, a vicious dictator who caused millions of deaths, and destruction all over Europe. He stopped at the English Channel, and destroyed his army in Russia, and finally was defeated by the British army at the Battle of Waterloo. But the War of 1812 extended into Canada and into the United States via the British Army and Navy.

Some historians classify the War of 1812 in America as an extension of the Revolutionary War. Most historians believe that the War of 1812 in the North was the act of the British to get the Indians to attack the settlers. They didn't care about the land tracts. Midwestern states such as Michigan and Ohio became the hot areas from the British soldiers, and the Indians to attack, and kill the settlers. Washington, D.C., and parts of Maryland were recaptured by the British. Washington was burning. Those were, for the most part, very cruel times. Some people had to fight hard to survive. During that time there were severe Indian wars going on in Indiana and Kentucky, because the Indians were fighting the Americans, siding with Tecumseh and the British. (There was another obscure episode in Maryland outside of Baltimore when Fort McHenry was being attacked by the British, Francis Scott Key from northern Maryland wrote the "The Star Spangled Banner," when he observed that the Americans held their positions, and the American flag was still flying the following day). General "Mad" Anthony Wayne went into northwestern Ohio hunting down the Indians, but went mad while the Indians were watching him, and finally did him in during the Battle of Falling Timbers, where the Indians cut a tree down upon General Wayne's tent, and crushed him.

The history of Ohio is interesting, because the original Inhabitants the "Eriez" (Western Iroquois) used it as a hunting ground. Lake Erie was good for fresh water, and fishing. Then the French set up trading posts before the Revolutionary War, then the British conquered them, and drove the French out, then General Washington surveyed the land, where southern Ohio was originally part of Virginia. George Washington also sent a few expeditions to the Ohio river all the way into Indiana to capture the British forts. After the Revolutionary War, the northern part of Ohio was called the Connecticut Land Co. The United States did not have any currency after the war. It was broke and Congress didn't know how to repay the soldiers from the war against the British, so they gave them land grants. Northern Ohio was part of that. But northwest Ohio was uninhabitable, because of the malarial swamps.

Geologically, Lake Erie was a remnant of what is known as a "Lacustrine Effect" front the last Ice Age, called the "Wisconsin." Lake Erie geologically is the oldest of the great lakes, and the most treacherous. As the ice receded 12,000 years ago, Lake Maumee, was long and wide. It extended into Illinois, and was reduced to Lake Warren, Whittlesee, and the Grand River formations to its present stage. There were many swamps upon the flat land after the lake kept on receding, and up until 200 years ago, the swamps existed on the flat lands known as the fire lands, where lots of German settlers were invited to come and drain the swamps, and turn the good land into organic, fertile soil excellent for agriculture. For most part, that area around lake Erie was biologically dangerous for humans. It caused encephalitis, if not that, the winters were severe, and along came the dampness. Anthropologically, the American Indians inhabited Ohio from approximately 10,000 years ago to 15,000 years ago. Some evidence of arthritis was found in some of the burial mounds, which meant that the climate was the same as it is now. There is evidence of glacial grooves of limestone scarped out by the glaciers, exposing the Ordovician limestone upon the western shore of Lake Erie.

CHAPTER ONE

THE LIFE AND TIMES OF OLIVER HAZARD PERRY

Some people have been brought into this life with the natural capability to lead. That is, they were born with it. Those individuals show a rare ability to perform under very stressful situations that can change the course of history. They seem to possess a greater tenacity than the average individual. Even when everything around them seems to fall apart, they find another way to work around it, by showing tact, and using every logical explanation available to them. Great leaders usually possess a strong character and hide their true emotions. These were the qualities that Oliver Hazard Perry showed with great strength, against lots of obstacles in his path.

War is a serious obstacle, so serious that the individual places himself in the line of fire, whether to live or to die, almost daily. It takes great leaders to move a navy, especially a few individuals placed in a grave situation, where they did not have any prior experience in any warfare command prior to the incident that took place on September 10, 1813 on Lake Erie. The reasons why they were chosen at that particular time, was because of other known incidents that confronted the individual, and his character.

The ancestry of a leader tells us the individual's make-up and his character reference. It also explains how the individual became good in his great works. The ancestry of Oliver Hazard Perry extends back into 17th-century England. All of the people that settled in the early colonies of America came from England. They were mainly individuals who were persecuted because of their religious beliefs. That was evident with the ancestry of Oliver Hazard Perry. Edmond Perry was the paternal 5th generation ancestor from Devonshire, England, in 1630. Public opinion was against the Quakers, which eventually led Edmond Perry to leave England by force, and to settle in South Kingston, Rhode Island, around Narragansett Bay. Rhode Island at that time had peaceful Indians remaining there, living amicably with the Europeans. The Narragansett tribe were kind and helpful to the new settlers, even though it was a beautiful hunting ground for their own survival. The Europeans had a harder and rougher time at survival though, because of the European life-style they were accustomed to. The European life-style was permanent, and less self-reliant compared to the new world. The colonies had to be built from scratch. Individuals became self-reliant to survive. Hunting, fishing, and log cutting were the duties of the day in the colonies. The weather was fierce at times, and individuals had to be hearty.

As time had passed, the colonies grew, and became self-reliant and sufficient enough to expand, with the help of slaves. With the backing of England's commerce, some of the colonists became wealthy. This was the case for the great grandson of Edmond Perry in Rhode Island. The colony of Rhode Island was comparable to Virginia for the wealthy land owners. The soil was tilled by slavery. The American society slowly but surely became luxurious, and attained refinements like that of England.

Freeman Perry was the great-grandson of Edmond, and became a lawyer. He retained great wealth, and married into a wealthy family, the daughter of Oliver Hazard. He became a judge of the court of common pleas, and a member of the colonial assembly. Freeman Perry was what we would call a proud patriot of the English colonies. His life was lived to the fullest. Christopher Raymond Perry, the third son of Freeman, was born on December 4, 1761. He was the father of Oliver Hazard Perry. The American Revolution broke out when Christopher was in his youth. He got involved in the defense of his country in the land and sea. He was a volunteer in the Kingston Reds, then later served aboard the sloop of war *Mifflin.* He became the second in command, He eventually was captured by the British, and was held for three months, and became infected with a contagious disease. After escaping, he served abroad the man of war *Trumbull,* which in turn got badly damaged.

At the conclusion of the war in 1783, Christopher continued sailing, and made trips to Europe, and on one particular voyage, he met his future wife, of Scottish decent. They were married in 1784 in Philadelphia, then proceeded back to Narragansett, Rhode Island to his father's home (Freeman Perry). His wife was welcomed into the Perry household as an exceptional member of the family, and on the 23rd of August, 1785, Oliver Hazard Perry was born. He was a frail child and exceptionally tall in his childhood, which some claim led to ill health. The climate, I feel, had a lot to do with making the child sickly, due to the damp weather. Oliver was not apparently a hearty child, but showed his pleasant side. There were a few incidents that he barely escaped with his life, and thank God for the understanding of the neighbors and friends who rescued him. He learned to read at a relatively young age, and when he was five years old, he attended his first school, where the schoolmaster was inherently lazy and misunderstood. Oliver didn't know quite what to make of him, because he taught the students while lying down upon a bed. As he grew older, he attended the school at Tower Hill, about four miles from his home, and used to walk. His first schoolmaster there was very old, and had previously taught his grandfather, Freeman.

As time went on, his father, a sea captain, made a great fortune overseas in Europe, South America, and the East Indies. When Christopher Perry arrived in Narragansett, Rhode Island, in 1794, he attained great wealth, then decided to move his family to Newport, Rhode Island. When Oliver began to attend the school in Newport, he had a mean and cruel schoolmaster named Mr. Frazer, who couldn't control his temper and would take his spite out on his students. There was an occasion when he became violent with Oliver, and hit his head, and severely hurt him. But Oliver's mother took action against the schoolmaster, and made him atone for it. Mr. Frazer was very intelligent, and personally instructed Oliver of the Application of Mathematics to Navigation, and Astronomy. Meanwhile, Oliver's family had grown to include four younger brothers and a sister. He and all of his brothers entered the naval service of their country. Mr. Frazer would take Oliver out to the beach along the Atlantic Ocean for a horizon to be obtained for astronomical observations, and taught Oliver the basic skills of navigation. A few years later Oliver became fascinated with book learning. He was well advanced for his age and became interested in Plutarch, Shakespeare and other philosophies at that time. In 1797, his father, Christopher, retired from the sea and moved his family to the village of Westerly Rhode Island.

Then in 1798, relations between the United States and France began to falter. Blaming it on the false involvement with the alliance during the Revolutionary War, France began to illegally obtain seamen to join their ranks against the British commerce. This was in terms destroying the British Neutrality, by using the United States to act against Britain. In 1798, Congress authorized 12 more ships of war to be included with the frigates the *United States*, the *Constitution*, and the *Constellation.* The ships of war were authorized to capture any French ships around the American shore, and to recapture any American vessel taken by the French. Oliver's father, Christopher, was invited to go to Warren, Rhode Island, for the construction of a ship named *General Greene* Since Oliver was the eldest, he at 13 years of age took over the household responsibility over all of the servants and the other children. He even paid the bills. He showed great maturity for his age, and commanded respect. He at times thought of himself as a great naval officer, especially in war games and, as his sister observed, he hated to lose.

A little after his 13th birthday, Oliver wrote to his father and asked for permission to join the U.S. Navy. It was granted and, at 14 years of age, he became a midshipman aboard the *General Greene* in 1799.

In 1796, France was entering into a disruptive environment in Europe which led to the "Reign of Terror," and to the execution of Louis XVI. This eventually led to the great soldier from Corsica finally to become the terror of Europe, Napoleon Bonaparte. This in turn ended the reign of terror by creating a dictatorship. Several events occurred in Europe which will be explained in future chapters which led England into the War of 1812. Eventually commerce was cut off completely against France all over Europe. England declared war on America. The United States became a victim from all sides.

Oliver Hazard Perry was slowly becoming educated, and getting prepared for what was in store for him in a certain moment in his life. Some say that it was an act of God, or just a matter of coincidence that the lad was living in the right environment for him, for what he eventually learned to love, and to take command of.

Author's Note: As previously mentioned, no matter how educated an individual becomes, it is not as important as the fact that the individual properly is trained at the right place and at the right moment for leadership. Chapter One contained few of the historical moments of Oliver Hazard Perry's life which led him to greatness. Since there was not enough written on him, I feel that he had normal behavior as other children in that time in history.

References

Brown, Arthur Wellington, *Library of Congress.*
Hoyt, Edwin Palmer, *The War of 1812.*

CHAPTER TWO

PRELUDE TO WAR

The final years of the 18th century looked bleak in the eyes of the Europeans, especially in France. America remained neutral, but wanted to continue to trade with the European merchants to survive. Things systematically fell apart during the turn of the century for all of Europe, with a terrible effect on England. Napoleon now had full control in France, but the war did not commence until 1802. By this time the French were driven out of the Caribbean by the British. Napoleon began to occupy Austria and Prussia, either by invasion or by just entering without conflicts. Austria was taken by marriage to his second wife, Maria Theresa. But the English began to resist the French, and at the Battle of Trafalgar in 1805, the Admiral Nelson defeated the French fleet. Napoleon was more of a land warrior, than that of a naval conqueror. Then by November 1806, Napoleon ordered all of the European ports closed to the British ships, which meant that England was cut off from the rest of Europe. Napoleon dominated almost every major seaport in Europe. That same year, Britain enforced a blockade of all incoming merchant ships, and all neutral ships had to obey the rules, including the Americans. But Britain could still survive with trade from their colonies especially in Canada.

America's entry into the War of 1812 was prompted by the British interference with American ships. The royal navy was actually stopping American ships from entering into European ports, and illegally searching American merchant ships at sea for British deserters. The British also began to impress Americans into the British army and, searching for deserters, made false accusations about individuals whom they thought to be from England. One problem in that case was the fact that the Americans were direct descendants of the British, and there was a similarity of facial features. The United States at that time fell victim to a circumstance that did not directly affect them. The United States was also self-sufficient, especially in agriculture. Agriculture was the main resource, though there was some industry. The U.S. could have stayed neutral until the war had ended with the downfall of Napoleon.

Author's Note: *Self reliance was the key for the American independence, before and during the Revolutionary War, especially in the realm of agriculture. The Americans used the issue of taxation to commence the Revolution against Britain. That is why, as stated earlier in the introduction, that most Americans considered the War of 1812 to be the second Revolutionary War.*

The War of 1812 was a so-called harassment and provoking by the British to get the Indians involved against the settlers.)

As time went on the conditions became worse for the Americans. The United States became an excellent scapegoat. But meanwhile the rest of Europe, including the British, were facing larger confrontations against Napoleon's army, The United States was a small confrontation for real military enforcement. During the spring of 1812, Napoleon declared war on Russia. This turned out to be the beginning of the end of his empire. His military victories were coming to an end with the invasion of Russia. He sent in hundreds of thousands of troops on a conquest that would destroy his entire army. Then on June 18, 1812, the United States Congress passed the legislation to declare war on England. Then on January 9, 1813, England declared war on the United States The problems America had was that there were very few army regulars and even fewer high-ranking officers, and all without proper training. The army was very small and disorganized. There was also another problem with declaring war. New England opposed going to war against their own countrymen because of trade. Western states such as Michigan, Ohio, and Kentucky favored war, and thought that they could fight cheaply. Congress gave President James Madison the right to draft from 10,000 to 35,000 men, and to request 50,000 men for one year, and 100,000 men for 6 months' service.

What the Americans in the western states did not realize was that the British intended to get the Indians to rise up against them, especially in western Ohio, Michigan and Indiana territories. The settlers in these states frequently got into small skirmishes with some Indians, because of the western movement. As the land was divided up and purchased by the settlers, the Indians were forced to move out. The American Indians had been there for millennia using the land as hunting grounds, which had no borders. A great leader emerged from the Shawnee tribe named Tecumseh. His mother was Creek Indian, and his father Shawnee. He had influence with the white people, and was educated enough to read Shakespeare and the Bible. He fell in love with Rebecca Galloway, she returned his affection, but wouldn't marry him unless he would turn from the Indian ways. That's when he decided to create a federation of Indian tribes to go against the white settlers. Tecumseh had a brother seven years younger, called Tenskwatawa, a medicine man known as the "Prophet." The Prophet was good for stirring up the tribe into a frenzy, and believing in the supernatural. But Tecumseh had excellent judgment of mankind and showed great leadership. He became radical, and had many followers who listened to him when he spoke of mistrust for the white settlers in America. He hoped for an alliance with the Choctaw, Chickasaw, Cherokee and the Creek tribes, but did not win them over for an alliance.

William Henry Harrison, Governor of the Territory of Indiana, decided to invade the Prophet's town to destroy Tecumseh. Tecumseh was not present during the Battle of Tippecanoe, when Harrison destroyed Prophetstown in 1811. This led Tecumseh to take the side of the British against the Americans. Harrison was also present during the Battle of Lake Erie. Harrison had lost 62 men, and 126 wounded. While General Jackson was pleased to hear of the news of the relenting barbarians, Harrison worried about an invasion from the Indians.

In the late months of 1812, the British Navy advanced up the St. Lawrence River into what was known as "Upper Canada." They maneuvered through the Lachine Rapids of the St. Lawrence onto Lake Ontario, which was smooth sailing, then onto Lake Erie. Upper Canada was a major area for the British army because of the access to the great lakes, and to make an alliance with the

Indians in that close proximity to invade the western states easily.

This prompted major shipbuilding activity for the British to control the Great Lakes, and to place the army. One problem the British had was that not all of the Canadians were sympathetic to their cause, especially the French Canadians in Quebec. In the beginning of the war, the Canadian economy began to boom, with more work than they could handle. War was actually declared on June 21, 1812, after the legislation passed the declaration on June 18, 1812. President Madison requested that Commodore Chauncey of the U.S. Navy investigate the northwestern Great Lakes region in the final months of 1812. This was just the beginning of the great showdown to come.

Authors Note: All of the facts that have been listed are considered to be the prelude to war, in the actual situations that occurred to create the alliances between the American Indians—the British, against the American settlers. Napoleon Bonaparte had been fighting since 1806 throughout Europe. When in 1812 was the beginning of the end for his empire, where the war had just begun for the United States.

References

Mahon, John K. *War of 1812*, pp. 20-23.
Turner, Wesley. *The War of 1812*, pp. 15-22.

CHAPTER THREE

THE ROAD TO WAR

In the beginning of the war, things were off to a cloudy start for the Americans. General Hull had surrendered to the British in Detroit, along with General Van Rensselaer at Niagara. This allowed the British to take complete control of Lake Erie all the way to the southern shores. General Harrison was in command of the northwestern army. He needed cooperation with the navy to set up a naval base for assistance in helping prevent a British invasion. On January 1, 1813, Commodore Chauncey stood on the east side of the great harbor area in Erie, Pennsylvania. Things seemed to look very grim, because the British had five armed vessels that had already sunk an American armed vessel, *Adams.* Captain Dobbins, a seasoned naval officer, lived to talk about how he escaped from the British then returned home to Erie, Pennsylvania. General Mead was at that time in command of Erie, Pennsylvania, and dispatched the news to Washington about the surrenders at Michelimackinack and Detroit. As soon as Captain Dobbins gave a report to President Madison, a special meeting was convened to prepare to build a fleet upon the shores of Lake Erie. Erie, Pennsylvania was to be the most suitable location for a naval station. In October, 1812, the first trees surrounding the Erie Harbor (Presque Isle) were felled in constructing the two sloops of war, the *Niagara*, and the *Lawrence.*

Captain Dobbins was waiting for the arrival of Commodore Chauncey, but Chauncey was too preoccupied with the lower lakes around Lake Ontario. The task of building a fleet was huge, and it was really difficult to find master carpenters. Dobbins had to go to New York to Black Rock, to find master carpenters and shipfitters. There was an abundance of oak and chestnut trees for the hull, and pine trees for the deck. The iron was imported from Pittsburgh, Pennsylvania. It was really expensive, and a long, tedious haul of 200 miles. Commodore Chauncey analyzed the situation of things taking place on that New Year's Day, and hoping to find himself a competent commander. Then on January 8, 1813, Commodore Chauncey went to Black Rock, New York, along the Niagara River to observe vessels being constructed for the squadron. A month later on February 8, 1813, Commodore Perry was requested to report to Sacketts Harbor. Commodore Oliver Hazard Perry wanted to take the command on the shores of Lake Erie. Commodore Chauncey was pleased to hear of this. Chauncey never knew Perry. But Perry had spent most of his life on the sea, with five of his brothers and two brother-in-laws, all of whom were part of the United States Navy.

This was going to be the fate of Commodore Perry, in which history reserved a special segment for him. However there was a certain incident in his past that did affect his career. Perry had left home to join his father on the *General Greene* in 1799. He became a midshipman at 14. By the time he was 17 years old, he had gotten promoted to lieutenant. When he was 20 years old, he became a captain of a schooner in the Mediterranean Sea. At 26, he was a captain on the gunboat *Revenge* in the Mediterranean Sea. In 1811, it struck a reef and several people were killed, but he was acquitted of the blame. But since that episode, shadows of bad luck seemed to haunt him. This was probably why he could not obtain a command on the sea. Besides, more important events were taking place on the sea during the war of 1812.

By March 3, 1813, Commodore Perry arrived in Sacketts Harbor. By March 27, 1813, Perry arrived in Erie, Pennsylvania at Presque Isle. The task that confronted him now was so enormous, the only way to deal with it was to work hard at it. There he already had the two sloops of war, the *Niagara* and the *Lawrence*. Those were his flagships that were well built for the showdown to come. These were built on the area around the Cascade Creek, just one mile west of Erie, The boat *Ariel* was built there. The gunboats *Porcupine*, *Tigress*, and *Scorpion* were built at the mouth of Leesrun, and thereafter a naval yard was constructed there, with one storehouse, and a hospital. Perry arrived in Sacketts Harbor, via Erie, Pennsylvania, with 100 experienced men from Newport, Rhode Island. Those were just the basic people he needed at that juncture.

Life in Erie was almost desolate. It was considered to be a frontier. The roads connecting to Pittsburgh were crude. It took a long time to drive wagons for 200 miles, hauling steel from Pittsburgh. By the end of March, 1813, the State of Pennsylvania sent him 500 militiamen to protect his naval establishment from any possible attacks from Indians or the British army. They stayed in the Presque Isle to defend it.

On March 30, 1813, Master Taylor arrived from Sacketts Harbor with 25 officers and placed them under the command of Perry, who was in Pittsburgh until April 7. On May 23, Perry and Dobbins left for Lake Ontario, and left Master Taylor in command. Four days later, Fort George along the Niagara River fell to the British, who completely evacuated the area. Then on June 13,

Perry ordered the immediate removal of the five vessels that were being built around Black Rock on the Niagara River into Lake Erie around Buffalo. They were the brig *Caledonia*, schooner *Somers*, sloop *Trippe*, schooner *Ohio*, schooner *Amelia*, they left for Erie, Pennsylvania the same day. They were each carrying 24-pound and 12-pound guns. Perry assumed that the British had a constant vigilance on any movement of vessels, but managed to pass by undetected because of the fog. The small fleet arrived at Presque Isle on June 19. Some people had assumed that the British were out to lunch, or at a dinner party in Canada to allow this to happen because the British controlled Lake Erie all the way to the south shores. Each of these vessels were 110 feet in length, 30 feet in width, with 9-foot hulls. Many people also assumed that the *Lawrence* was named after the St. Lawrence River. The *Niagara* was named after the Niagara River, but the *Lawrence* was named after Capt. James Lawrence, who was killed while in command of the Chesapeake during an encounter with the British. Perry also adopted Captain Lawrence's famous last words: "Don't give up the ship" for a motto for his battle flag.

The British fleet consisted of *Queen Charlotte*, *Lady Provost*, *Hunter*, *Little Belt*, and *Chippewa*. On June 24, the *Lawrence* was completed, and the *Niagara* on July 4, 1813. All Perry lacked was a crew. Perry had only 490 men, and needed a total of 740. In April, 1813, the British sent Captain Robert Heriot Barclay from England to Quebec. He was supposed to arrive in February, but was delayed by bad weather. On May 9, he was in Kingston along the shores of Lake Ontario but was eventually superseded by Sir James Yeo to take command on Lake Erie, after Captain Mulcaster declined the offer. Barclay sailed on the vessels *Lady Provost*, and the *Chippewa*, which took him to Amherstburg. Barclay had problems with the shortage of supplies, and manpower. Another problem was to prevent Perry from combining his vessels from Black Rock to Presque Isle. But he allowed that to slip by him.

On July 16, Barclay asked General Procter for 500 soldiers and 1000 Indians from Procter's command, but he could not provide them without reinforcements for himself. Barclay then remained in Presque Isle with a military blockade surrounding Perry's fleet. Sand bars prevented Barclay from entering into Presque Isle—the deepest part of Presque Isle was only six feet deep.

Perry had a serious problem at Presque Isle. The inner harbor was too shallow for the *Niagara*, and the *Lawrence* to sail out into the lake. The hulls were too deep to get through the sand bars.

But during the two-week blockade by the British there were a few times that there was an exchange of fire, which really didn't do much damage. Barclay wanted to attack right there at Presque Isle, but couldn't, due to the shortage of manpower and supplies. Then by July 31, Barclay's fleet disappeared, and no one knew why. Perry also had another problem with the 125 men that Commodore Chauncey sent him—he complained that they were a motley crew that consisted of blacks, boys, and soldiers. Perry didn't seem to think that Chauncey had even looked at them. Chauncey's reply was sharp, saying, "I regret that you are not pleased with them, for to my knowledge a part of them are not surpassed by any seamen we have in a fleet, and I have yet to learn the color of the skin, or the cut and trimmings of the coat can affect the a man's qualifications or usefulness." This letter was delivered by Jesse D. Elliot. The letter went on, and was insulting to Perry. Perry's reply was a request to be relieved. Chauncey became apologetic. Others interceded, and Perry was persuaded to remain. Between August 1, and August 4, it took a day and a night to get the *Lawrence* out past the sandbars without the armament, and using camels (sunken watertight boxes filled up then emptied out).

The *Lawrence* was the first to float out. It was rearmoured, and it covered the passage of the other five vessels. The following came the *Niagara*. By that time Barclay's flotilla had arrived, right after Perry's fleet entered into the lake. Barclay's reaction was that he was outnumbered as he observed the entire American fleet enter the lake, and that was why he could not attack them at once. Captain Barclay's image did not look very good in his present command, because of the lack of support from the British command. Barclay had an established reputation in the wars against Napoleon at Trafalgar, where he had lost an arm. To arm the *Detroit* with 21 guns, he stripped the fort at Amherstburg. Barclay had about 440 men. Perry, had only 530 men, mostly Kentucky marksmen from General Harrison. On August 10, Lieutenant Elliot was to be admitted to Perry's fleet, and the vessel *Ariel* was to pick him up on the way to the head of Lake Erie towards Sandusky Bay. Elliot brought 90 seamen and a number of officers. Around August 21, Perry, in conjunction with General Harrison, chose Put-In-Bay on Gibraltar Island for his new base. Barclay chose the Detroit River as the British base.

On August 27, Perry became ill with lake fever, which infected at least 30 of his men on each vessel. Even though he was prepared to attack, the fever delayed the attack by two weeks. Another underlying problem for Perry was an officer that had just arrived with ulterior motives for himself. This particular individual was willing in every way to discredit Commodore Perry. Even then in early years of the 19th century human emotions came out as they do in the 20th century.

Author's Note: The motives of Lieutenant Elliot were never concluded historically, but his behavior gave the impression that he wanted the limelight for himself. He hoped that Perry would be defeated by death in the line of duty, or disgraced by surrender. We will see during the "Showdown on Lake Erie," many indications of Elliot's true nature.

References

Mahon, John K., The War of 1812, pp. 165-171.

Mills, James, Erie Battle of 1813.

Paullin, Charles, Erie Lake Battle of 1813.

CHAPTER FOUR

INVASION DAY

On September 6, 1813, Barclay maneuvered six of his ships out into the lake. He was aboard the *Detroit*, with 19 guns and 2 howitzers. The *Queen Charlotte* with 17 guns, one howitzer; schooner *Lady Prevost* with 13 guns and one howitzer; brig *Hunter*, with 10 guns; sloop *Little Belt*, with three guns; and schooner *Chippewa* with one gun, and 2 swivels. Perry expected seven ships, but the *Erie* never emerged. The six British ships threw a broadside of 459 pounds, 195 of them from the long guns. The 9 Americans threw a broadside with 896 pounds, 288 of them from the long guns. Barclay knew that his was inferior.

Perry called a gathering of officers on the evening of September 9. Perry discussed the battle plans, for he did not know that Barclay had sailed, and ordered each ship commander to fire at close range, and to watch for the signal to attack. It was a large blue pennant with white letters with the motto "Don't give up the ship." Once this pennant was displayed on his ship, that was the signal for attack.

At dawn on September 10, 1813, the British fleet was sighted coming in from the northwest. Perry excitedly told his crew to fight from the windward or the leeward side, because the wind was coming in from the northwest to the southeast.

About nine miles from Put-In-Bay, Barclay hove to and fro, then remained stationary facing the southwest. Barclay was waiting for the impact. The *Detroit* was second in the British line. Perry signaled for Elliot to drop from second place to third place on the *Niagara.* This maneuver would get the *Lawrence* to close in with the *Detroit*, and the *Niagara* would close in with the *Queen Charlotte,* which was fourth in the British line. The *Somers, Porcupine, Tigress,* and *Trippe* were a mile behind the *Lawrence.* These vessels behind the *Lawrence* were also ordered to engage the first British ship as they came up. Around 10:30 a.m., another breeze came up, and all bore close to a gallant formation to meet the enemy. Perry raised the battle flag, then immediately followed by three ringing cheers. These were the moments of Perry's life where time stood still. All his nerves were on edge. This was a matter of life, and death, and the fate of the United States of America. At approximately 11:45 a.m., on September 10, 1813, the British bugle sounded on the *Detroit*, followed by the playing of "Rule Britannia," then followed by the first shot coming from the *Detroit*, which was a miss as it fired towards the *Lawrence.* They were about a mile and a half from each other, facing at a 25-degree angle. The *Lawrence* fired back, and the Battle of Lake Erie was joined.

Commodore Perry's younger brother was present during this conflict, along with an American Indian from Rhode Island, who was a friend of Perry's. He wanted to follow him into the conflict. All of the British guns were ordered to fire at once. Perry ordered the *Scorpion* to fire, then the *Ariel*, then the *Lawrence* began to fire, then the *Caledonia* fired again against the *Queen Charlotte*. The *Lawrence* was the main target for all of the British guns all at once. For two solid hours, the *Detroit*, *Queen Charlotte*, and the *Hunter* concentrated on the *Lawrence*. One by one, every officer fell right in front of Perry. The American vessels from the rear had not closed in. The *Caledonia*, *Ariel*, and the *Scorpion*, were also heavily engaged. The *Niagara* under the command of Lieutenant Elliot, was the only vessel that didn't contribute effectively in the battle. The *Lawrence* began with a total of 100 men, and after two hours of fighting 21 men had died, with 63 wounded. The *Niagara* didn't close in with the *Queen Charlotte*, but was effective with the two long guns. When Perry's battleship, the *Lawrence*, was destroyed, he abandoned it and stood up in a rowboat with four or five crewmen. This was a moralistic statement coming from Perry, showing the he was still fighting even as he abandoned the *Lawrence*. Barclay sighted Perry, but really could not identify him clearly, and the British began to take shots towards him, as his crewmen pulled him down to prevent him from getting shot.

Perry was unhurt, but then as he boarded the *Niagara* he came face to face with Elliot, and a few choice words were exchanged. Elliot's version was that Perry blurted out, "The day is lost!" Elliot then reassured him and added, "Take charge of my battery while I bring the boats in close action, and the day will yet be ours." Elliot next rowed from schooner to schooner in much greater danger than Perry had been and ordered them forward. They obeyed him, and their fire won the battle. Elliot returned then to the *Niagara*, and Perry supposedly said, "I owe all of this to your exertions."

This was one of the problems Perry had with Elliot, when Elliot attempted to discredit him. It wasn't in Perry's character to say these things or act upon them. Perry was never known to lose his composure. Elliot did leave the *Niagara* and rowed towards the schooners. Later the balance of the battle tipped in the favor of the Americans. Perry fired from the *Niagara* at *Lady Prevost, Little Belt,* and *Chippewa*, from the starboard side, then from the starboard side fired at the broadside at the *Detroit*, and the *Queen Charlotte*. Barclay's remaining arm was hit, and then every British ship's commander was killed. The *Lawrence* had to surrender, because it was badly riddled with bullets. There was a rumor among the British that Perry actually did surrender, but they continued to fight. At 4:00 p.m. on September 10, 1813, Perry returned to the *Lawrence* to accept the British surrender.

With his sword raised with his right arm, Perry stood straight up and accepted the surrender as he approached the *Detroit.* The human cost of the conflict was 44 British and 21 Americans killed in action, with 103 British and 63 Americans wounded. Perry composed two victory messages. The first one, to Secretary Jones said, "It has pleased the Almighty to give to the arms of the United States a signal victory over their enemies on this lake. The British squadron consisting of two ships, two brigs, one schooner, and a sloop, have at this moment surrendered to the force under my command after a sharp conflict." The message to General Harrison was more powerful: "We have met the enemy, and they are ours—two ships, two brigs, one schooner, and a sloop."

Perry's victory swept up the control over the entire lake, and took it from the British. This was the first real victory for the Americans during the War of 1812. Captains Barclay and Prevost blamed the defeat on Commodore Yeo for not reinforcing them, but the battle was unavoidable. The Earl of

Bathurst read about the defeat on November 4, 1813, and wanted to re-establish another British fleet upon Lake Erie. A British magazine informed its readers that the Americans had defeated not the British Navy, but a local Canadian organization. The War of 1812 in America paled in comparison to the fighting against Napoleon. Five weeks following the Battle of Lake Erie, a huge battle in Leipzig, Germany, involved 2,000 cannons, and 500,000 men. Lake Erie involved 15 small ships with 970 men.

Commodore Perry became a great hero across the United States. Large businesses began to profit from this victory, and Perry became a national hero even to his Grandfather Freeman Perry, who at 85 years of age lived to see his grandson's glory. Commodore Perry received a huge victory celebration when he arrived back in Eric, Pennsylvania, and there were others all over the country. Perry received three months' advance pay of $7,000, and several medals. General Harrison became ecstatic, because this paved the way for the U.S. Army to retake Detroit and the Michelimackinac from the British, and Indians.

In 1818, the year the shares were paid, Elliot made an offensive communication to Perry. Perry replied "You reduce me to the necessity of reminding you of the abject condition in which I previously found you...sick or pretending to be sick in bed within consequence of distress in mind. The reputation you have lost was tarnished by your own behavior on Lake Erie. Mean and despicable as you have proved yourself to be, I shall never cease to criminate myself for screening you from public contempt."

A year after the British defeat on Lake Erie, Captain Barclay was up against a court martial. But charges were dropped, because he didn't have the proper means for his support. He lacked supplies; most of his seasoned officers were killed right away; each vessel had no more than 10 seasoned officers; the cannons were defective; and Barclay's leadership was withdrawn because of wounds. Lieutenant Elliot was given the command to take over the navy on Lake Erie, while Perry returned to Rhode Island. Perry was going to have him court martialed, but the case was withdrawn. Then Elliot wanted to have a duel with Perry. Perry claimed that he was a staunch Jacksonian and was persecuted by the consequences of Republican principles.

Authors note: Everything mentioned here was taken from the actual documents from the Library of Congress, and <u>The War of 1812,</u> by John K. Mahon. Commodore Perry's actual statement were taken verbatim, and not intended as plagiarism. Statements made by the individuals are to be taken word for word to show evidence of what was actually said.

Reference

Mahon, John K., *The War of 1812*, pp. 173-177.

Mills, James, *Erie Battle of 1813*.

Paullin, Charles, *Erie Lake Battle of 1813*.

CHAPTER FIVE

THE AFTERMATH

During the Battle of Lake Erie, Commodore Barclay was seriously wounded, and Perry had sympathy for him and all the men who had been wounded. While the dead sailors were buried at the scene of the conflict, the officers were taken to Put-In-Bay to be buried on September 11. The Americans and British marched together for the funeral procession with the bands playing, after which a volley of muskets was fired. The badly wounded were taken upon the *Lawrence* to Erie, Pennsylvania.

On September 20, 1813, the *Lawrence* was sent to Erie, Pennsylvania, and following it were the British *Detroit* and *Queen Charlotte*. Other vessels were used to transport 3,500 Kentucky volunteers into the Middle Bass Islands, then on the 27th into Canada. Perry acted as an aide to General Harrison in Detroit until he received new orders. In October, Perry received orders from the Secretary of the Navy (Jones) promoting him to Post Captain, and was granting him leave time. On October 20, Perry returned to Put-In-Bay upon the *Ariel*, retrieved Captain Barclay with his surgeon, and sailed upon the *Ariel* to Erie, Pennsylvania. Perry secured a pardon for Captain Barclay, and transportation for him to return to England. On October 23, Perry sailed upon the *Ariel* to Buffalo, New York, after receiving a grand reception in Erie for his victory, he then returned to his home in Rhode Island.

What happened to the entire fleet was sort of interesting. The *Detroit* and *Queen Charlotte* were wintered in Put-In-Bay, and the *Tigress* was sent to protect them. The *Ariel* and *Chippewa* were sent to Buffalo, New York, but parted cable and went adrift, and completely lost. The *Trippe*, and *Little Belt* were wintered in Black Rock around Buffalo, and were eventually burned by the British when they invaded Buffalo that winter. The *Somers* went to Put-In-Bay, and *Ohio* went to Erie, Pennsylvania. In 1815 the *Detroit*, *Queen Charlotte*, and the *Lawrence* were sunk in Misery Bay in Presque Isle, Erie, Pennsylvania. The *Niagara* was kept afloat. In 1820, the naval station was in a state of reduction, then by 1826 the station was sold. Benjamin Brown bought the *Niagara*, *Queen Charlotte*, *Lawrence*, and the *Detroit*, then sold them to Captain Miles in 1836, but the *Lawrence* was too badly damaged, and was left sunk in Misery Bay. A few years later the *Niagara* was sunk in Misery Bay. By 1876, the *Lawrence* was raised, and sent to an exhibition in Philadelphia, but then it got burned. In 1913, the *Niagara* got raised from Misery Bay, and put on display for the 100th anniversary of the Battle of Lake Erie.

Five weeks after the Battle of Lake Erie was Napoleon's final assault, where he was headed for disaster. Napoleon was defeated in Russia in the attempt to take Moscow, when he was outwitted by the Russians. Then the Russians followed Napoleon on the great retreat towards Germany. The British Army and the Prussians waited for him. There were hundreds of thousands of men, and thousands of cannons—the British put all of their war efforts into the defeat of Napoleon. The conflict with the United States was placed on the back burner for the time being, until the British had control over the situation in Europe. Napoleon finally had to take refuge west of the Rhine River where he would be driven to final defeat.

On August 19, 1814, the British Major General Robert Ross landed on the Patuxent River in the state of Maryland, and followed the good roads along the river. The incompetence of the Americans destroyed their own boats, and when the British were marching along, they were not attacked. By the time the British arrived in Bladensburg, the American defenders ran away and allowed the British to attack Washington, D.C. This was called the "Bladensburg Races." The inside of the president's home was burning, but the outside was left intact. Therefore, instead of immediately repairing anything, the walls were painted with whitewash. The president's home from that time on was called the "White House." The Bladensburg Races allowed General Ross to invade Baltimore on his way up the Chesapeake Bay. On September 13 and 14, 1814, Ft. McHenry in Baltimore was attacked, with four killed and 24 wounded. Francis Scott Key, who was serving in the military aboard the cartel ship, *Minden*, observed the battle all night long and he wrote a poem about the "Star-Spangled Banner." The Americans held up against the British there. But the war raged on along with the states of Ohio, Kentucky, and Tennessee still being the main activists against the British.

During the final months of 1813, Commodore Perry was enjoying the life of a hero, and of an American Naval officer. He lived the good life with his wife and children in Newport Rhode Island, and enjoyed the parties and the respect that came along with it. After he left Buffalo, New York, Captain Elliot resumed the command of the U.S. Navy on Lake Erie. But he still had resentful feelings against the charges that Perry had made. Elliot gave his side of the story, but hung onto those feelings. Realistically, Elliot did his share of the fighting, but not to Perry's expectations when they were required at the proper moment. But history really doesn't know if he was jealous of Perry. Elliot eventually wanted to have a duel against Perry, but Perry wanted Elliot to be court martialed. In 1818, Commodore Chauncey set up the proceedings for a court martial hearing involving Perry. But other events intervened during the long, dragged-out war.

The American navy, during 1814, was still being harassed by the British until the end of the war. It was also being harassed by the Dey of Algiers in the Mediterranean Sea. The war ended officially on December 24, 1814, but word didn't reach General Andrew Jackson during the Battle of New Orleans in January, 1815. There were too many navy heroes at the end of the war, which was called "The War that Nobody Really Won."

On August 5, 1815, Commodore Perry was assigned to the frigate *Java* at Hampton Roads, Virginia. In December, 1815, the navy decided to send Perry to the Mediterranean. Perry almost lost his life in the process of sailing the *Java*, due to terrible storms in the Atlantic. On March 7, 1816, the *Java*, along with the *Ontario* and the *Erie*, sailed for Algiers, and to make the Dey of Algiers surrender, and for the Americans to take control of the shores of Tripoli. The Americans were to capture the Algerian Navy, and to create and sign a new treaty with them. There again, Commodore Perry had some troubles with a United States Marine Corps detachment upon his vessel.

Perry was an upright, conservative gentleman, and not used to rowdy marines, including the Captain Heath, who was a drunken, loudmouthed upstart. Heath decided to jump ship, and Perry ordered him to be relieved of command. Perry had no official capacity to do that, but took it upon himself for the sake of respect. Before leaving the Mediterranean, there was an outbreak of smallpox and seven of Perry's men died returning to Rhode Island.

During the spring of 1815, Captain Elliot decided to hold a mock court martial in New York Harbor against Commodore Perry upon the frigate *Ontario*, but nothing came of it. By 1817, Captain Heath and Elliot were planning to blacken Perry's reputation, but failed. Heath then had a duel against Perry, where Heath shot first, and missed. When Perry was to shoot, he laid his pistol down and refused to lower himself for that purpose. (On October 19, Aaron Burr killed Alexander Hamilton in a duel in Hoboken, New Jersey.)

In 1817, President James Monroe came to visit New England and rescue Perry from his troubles. I personally feel that there were petty jealousies, and a bitterness between Perry and Elliot. At that time, the military could not enforce proper discipline as they do in the 20th century. President Monroe personally asked Perry to be his personal aide and to survey the battleship *Independence* and to survey the entrance to the Long Island Sound. The navy was not a generous employer— one did not work unless there was some specific job to be fulfilled. By 1818-1819 there was the States Rights Act that permitted each state to defend itself against any aggression. In the spring of 1819, Perry was sent to New York to do a job for the federal government by the Secretary of the Navy, Smith Thompson. This was to be a delicate mission to Venezuela, which was at war with Spain. Perry was to sail on the sloop *John Adams.* The *Constellation* followed, and they had a rough time in the Caribbean, because everything was uncharted. They arrived in Barbados on July 5, and Perry transferred to the *Nonesuch,* sending the *John Adams* to the Port of Spain, 150 miles away. On July 26, Antonio Francisco Zea greeted the *Nonesuch* (Simon Bolivar was fighting the War of Independence elsewhere). On July 28, Perry had an informal meeting with the vice president. Perry stayed with an American, Dr. Forsythe, who lived in Venezuela. On August 11, 1819, Perry was assured that he could leave, but had a serious problem on his ships, because the crews were sick with yellow fever. On August 14, 1819, there was a dinner given in Commodore Perry's honor, but that night aboard ship, he complained of having a headache and low spirits.

The *Nonesuch* was stranded on the Orinoco River when Perry became really ill and burning up with a fever. On his deathbed, he gave an oral command to bequeath all of his estates to his wife.

On his 34th birthday, August 23rd 1819, Commodore Perry had a vomiting attack and was so weak he laid down and died. Three days later the *Nonesuch* reached the mouth of the Orinoco River, where he was taken ashore to be buried.

Since yellow fever was a dreaded disease and no one at that time knew how it was contracted, Perry had to remain in the Caribbean area. He had a full military dirge, joined by the British navy which had some sailors in the Caribbean who had fought in the Battle of Lake Erie. They remembered how Perry treated them after they, the British, had surrendered. Oliver Hazard Perry was buried on the Island of Trinidad, though in 1826 his remains were transferred to Newport, Rhode Island.

The last survivor of Perry's crew was named Benjamin Fleming who resided in Erie, Pennsylvania. In 1860 Fleming went to a monument in Cleveland, Ohio, commemorating the Battle of Lake Erie. Fleming was well known throughout the Erie area. Mr. Fleming died at the age of 96 in 1870 in Erie. Fleming talked over and over about how Perry used sand upon the planks so that the blood would be stopped. At his death, his body lay in state in the courthouse in Erie, where hundreds of people came to see the last survivor of the Battle of Lake Erie.

Author's Note: In conclusion, the tragic story of the life, and the times of Commodore Oliver Hazard Perry, was a sad one. But I feel that some men are predestined into greatness. During the early years of the 19th century, life in itself was meager, and the chances of survival were not very high. This also depicts the ideas of men remain the same, including the deadly sins of emotions— Hate, Jealousy, Envy, Greed, Resentment, etc. The War of 1812 was eventually forgotten in the modern annals of history. It became the back-burner petty war of little importance. I thought of a famous individual who actually participated to the freedom and the greatness of the United States of America. Time has forgotten these heroes.

Reference

Hoyt, Edwin Palmer, The Tragic Commodore, pp. 125-155.

Mahon, John K., The War of 1812, pp. 307-309.

Paullin, Charles, <u>Erie Lake Battle of 1813</u>.

Turner, Wesley, <u>The War of 1812: The War That Both Sides Won</u>, pp. 108-109, 175.